Ninja Foodi Smart Xl Grill

A Modern Guide To Master The Art Of Indoor Grilling And Air Frying With These New And Yummy Recipes Beginners Can Try At Home

Lilla Marcus

Table of Contents

Introduction

N inja Foodi XL Grill Cookbook" introduces you to the Ninja Foodi XL grill and provides you with over 2000 healthy recipes created only for this grill. The book will show you how to prepare a variety of delicious dishes with this versatile grill.

This is the food processor that I have been waiting for since I started cooking. Its large capacity bowl and versatile blade assembly make it an ideal product to use for everyday cooking.

Foodi Smart XL Grill, the latest kitchen appliance by Ninja Foodi, is a food processor that can be used as a griller, slicer, mixer, and blender at homes.

Foodi Smart XL has a large processing bowl of 6.4 quarts capacity that can hold a lot of food for slicing or grilling. The bowl is large enough to make ten servings of coleslaw or salsa, and it is the perfect size for roasting a 3-pound chicken as well.

And the blade assembly can chop, slice shred, mix and blend.

The cookbook starts with an introduction to the Ninja Foodi XL grill. You will learn how to clean the grill, prepare it for use, and then go through the instructions for using this amazing kitchen appliance.

After reading "Ninja Foodi XL Grill Cookbook", you will be ready to make healthy and delicious dishes. You can use this book as a great reference guide for all your grill cooking needs. It can also be a significant learning experience for those who want to get inspired to cook new dishes or gain cooking skills.

When cooking at home, you want a cookbook that delivers. Every cookbook should be tailored to your specific needs, so why not designed for the Ninja Foodi XL Grill? The same team is written by Ninja Foodie XL Grill Cookbook's Ninja Foodie XL Grill Cookbook 1-2-3 series. The Ninja Foodi XL Grill Cookbook offers a practical approach to grilling that will help you get the most from your new grill.

Previous grills have either been too small or not easy to use. I wanted to create the perfect healthy alternative for my family, so I worked on creating a healthier way to cook and grill.

But my mission wasn't only to create a healthy way of cooking but to also make it easy for everyone.

With Ninja Foodi Smart XL Grill everything is easier, and you will be able to enjoy your favorite grilled food with less work and hassle.

While all of our cookbooks provide a great foundation for your grilling adventures, this one is specially designed for this recent addition to the Ninja Foodi XL Grill Cookbook family. We love our Ninja Foodi XL Grill, so we took extra time to make sure we offered the best possible guidance on its proper use.

The Ninja Foodi grill and the other grills differ in several ways. The enormous difference is that the Ninja Foodi Grill heats faster than other grills and cooks much more evenly. This is because the Ninja Foodi Smart XL grill is a solid core-less infrared grill. It uses ceramic infrared burners, which are in a cylinder inside the grill, therefore there are no gaps between the heating elements (unlike most electric grills).

Whether you are a first-time griller or a seasoned pro, The Ninja Foodie XL Grill Cookbook delivers the information you need to ensure that your time spent on the grill will reward and pleasurable.

CHAPTER 1:

Six Methods of Ninja Foodi XL Smart Grill

Now that you have a basic idea of what the Ninja Foodi Smart XL Grill is let's look at the core functions and buttons you should know about. Remember that you have five different cooking types that you can do using your Ninja Foodi Grill.

Grill

At its heart, the Ninja Foodi Smart XL Grill is an indoor grill, so to unlock its full potential, you must understand how the grill function of the appliance works. Let me break it down to you.

Now understand that each set of the Grill is specifically designed for fresh food.

But regardless of which function you choose, the first step for you will always be:

- Place your cooking pot and grill grate in the Ninja Foodi.'
- Let it pre-heat
- Then add your food

The next thing would be to select the Grill function and choose the Grill Temperature. Here you have 4 settings to choose from.

- **Low:** This mode is perfect for bacon and sausages.
- **Medium:** This is perfect for frozen meats or marinated meats.
- **High:** This mode is perfect for steaks, chicken, and burgers.
- **Max:** This is perfect for vegetables, fruits, fresh and frozen seafood, and pizza.

Air Crisp

The Air Crisp mode will help you achieve a very crispy and crunchy golden-brown finish to your food. Using the Air Crisp mode combined with the crisper basket is the perfect combination to cook frozen foods such as french fries, onion rings, and chicken nuggets. Air Crisp is also amazing for Brussels sprouts and other fresh vegetables. Just always shake the crisper basket once or twice to ensure even cooking.

Bake

As mentioned earlier, the Ninja Foodi Smart XL Grill is essentially a mini convection oven. All you need to bake bread, cakes, pies, and other sweet treats is a Cooking Pot and this function. The Pre-heat time for the Bake mode is just 3 minutes.

Roast

The Roast function is used to make everything from slow-roasted pot roast to appetizers to casual sides. Large protein pieces can be put directly in your Ninja Foodi Smart XL Grill and roasted using this function. You can further make this mode more effective by using a Roasting Rack accessory.

Dehydrate

Dehydrators are pretty expensive and take a lot of space in your kitchen. Luckily, you can very easily dehydrate fruits, meats, vegetables, herbs, etc., using just your Ninja Foodi Grill!

The Inspiration Behind This Cookbook

One of my all-time favorite foods is Beef Stew. It's a great meal to batch cook for those busy nights, but it's also what I make for my kids when they're sick. Beef stew is not only hearty and delicious, but it reminds me of my childhood in a way that could bring me to tears. Now, before my Ninja Foodi… Let me tell you how I used to make Beef Stew. First, I would pat dry the beef cubes and season them - this step is a no brainer. Next, I would heat a frying pan on high with some oil and slowly sear the beef, in batches so I didn't overcrowd the pan. It takes a long time and produces a lot of smoke, not to mention, using a lot of oil. Next, I would fill my slow cooker with stock and vegetables. This worked great but took all day to cook and created a lot of dishes to clean.

With the Ninja Foodi, I can sear, simmer, roast, and braise all in one easy-to-clean appliance. The pre-programmed buttons make it so easy, even my kids can make beef stew in it now! This is one of the tabletop appliances on the market that gets hot enough to sear meat properly, so the first thing I made with my Ninja Foodi was beef stew.

What Makes the Ninja Foodi so Great?

Authorization strolls you through how I make beef stew since getting my Ninja Foodi. I open a package of meat, season it, and add it to the Ninja foodi and set it to "sear." In minutes, the temperature has reached 500F so I set a timer after placing the lid on (so there's virtually no smoke at all,) and then come back when the timer has gone off to add the stock and fresh veggies... And voila! In just one hour I have tender, flavorful, juicy, hearty, healthy beef stew!

But it's more than just beef stew! I use my Ninja Foodi for just about everything now, which is why I wanted to create this cookbook (with more than 500 recipes!) to show you how you too can revolutionize the way you cook. You and your family will save time and be healthier in the end - it's really a win-win! (You might also end up feeling like a world-class chef in the end, because everything in this book is so tasty!)

Along with saving money on my energy bill and saving me tons of time around dinner time, this appliance also helped make me and my family healthier! I used to add a lot of oil to the surface of meat before cooking, to prevent it from sticking. I was fed up with losing half a chicken breast on the barbeque so then I started baking them, which didn't offer a lot of flavors. I also used a lot of oil on things like grilled bread, fish, or vegetables. But with the air crisp setting on this machine, you don't need to use any oil whatsoever... which has had an incredible impact on my health. If you're not concerned about oil, this machine will still allow you to enjoy more of the foods that fit into your meal plan – for keto or paleo diets, the Ninja Foodi is a great addition to your kitchen, because of how conveniently you can cook such a variety of proteins.

Making the Most of Your Ninja Foodi

The Ninja Foodi has 6 function buttons which completely replaced my toaster, toaster oven, deep fryer, oven, stovetop, microwave, and even my outdoor barbeque! With this device, I can roast a chicken, a whole fish, or any of my favorite oven meals. I can quickly heat up a piece of pizza or toast. I can air crisp chicken wings or fish sticks for the kids. I can bake a cake or fresh bread. I can dehydrate apple chips or kale chips. I can broil garlic bread or grilled cheese. And probably most impressively... I can grill with no smoke or fire hazards year-round indoors!! Now you try to name an appliance that can do all of that!?!?!

Now you may be wondering – "But is this thing really as good as my barbeque?" The answer is YES and once you try just a few of the recipes from this cook, you will see for yourself. So far, I have grilled everything from shrimp skewers to corn on the cob, to loaded baked potatoes, to hot dogs and yes, even the perfect medium-rare steak. The Ninja Foodi comes with a thermometer probe that is inserted into the center of a seasoned steak, to alert you when it's reached your desire doneness. Once the internal temperature of the steak reaches that temperature, you open the lid and have the perfectly cooked dinner. It really is that easy! Alongside your steak, you can also enjoy perfectly roasted vegetables and potatoes, and you can even enjoy a fresh-baked apple pie for dessert… all from your Ninja Foodi!

One of the finest parts of this machine though is that it reaches a temperature of 500F – this is almost unheard of for a tabletop interior grill. This high temperature allows me to properly sear my food (especially steaks, chicken, or fish) and really allows it to get those tasty grill marks. But this device does more than just sear, as I've told you… because of its unique cyclonic technology, it also circulates the air around your food continuously, which cooks food perfectly, every time.

Ninja Foodi Smart XL Grill

Characteristics	Ninja Foodi AG301 Grill	Ninja Foodi Smart XL Grill
Cooking programs	There are five cook programs. Grill, Air crisp, Bake, Roast, and Dehydrate.	There are six cook programs. Broil, Dehydrate, Air crisp, Roast, Bake, and Grill.
Smart temperature probe	Absent. You have to rely a bit on guesswork to attain that perfect doneness.	Dual sensor Present. To continuously monitor the temperature accuracy for even more perfect doneness. Multi-task away since it cancels the need to watch over the food.
Smart cook system	Absent. Requires frequent checks and guesswork for satisfactory results.	Present. With 4 smart protein settings and 9 customizable doneness levels, all the work is done to input the required setting. Just wait for your food to cook. You could be busy doing your laundry while you cook.
Weight	20 pounds	27.5 pounds
Dimension (L×W×H) inches	12.5 ×16.88×10.59 inches.	18.8 x 17.7 x 14 inches. Therefore, this is the larger option for large-sized family dishes and 50% more grilling space.

CHAPTER 2:

Breakfast Recipes

1. Cheese Toasts with Eggs & Bacon

Preparation Time: 10 mins

Cooking Time: 4 mins

Servings: 2

Ingredients:

- 4 bread slices

- 1 garlic clove, minced

- 4 ounces goat cheese, crumbled

- Freshly ground black pepper, to taste

- 2 hard-boiled eggs, peeled and chopped

4 cooked bacon slices, crumbled

Directions:

1. In a food processor, add the garlic, ricotta, lemon zest and black pepper and pulse until smooth.

2. Spread ricotta mixture over each bread slices evenly.

3. Press "Power" button of Ninja Foodi Digital Air Fry Oven and turn the dial to select "Air Fry" mode.

4. Press "Time" button and again turn the dial to set the cooking time to 4 minutes.

5. Now push "Temp" button and rotate the dial to set the temperature at 355 degrees F.

6. Press "Start/Pause" button to start.

7. When the unit beeps to show that it is preheated, open the lid and lightly, grease the sheet pan.

8. Arrange the bread slices into the sheet pan and insert in the oven.

9. When the unit beeps to show that cooking time is completed, press "Power" button to stop cooking and open the lid.

10. Divide bread slices onto serving plates.

11. Top with bacon pieces and serve alongside eggs.

Nutrition:

- Calories: 416 Fat: 29.2g

- Saturated Fat 16.9g Trans Fat: 12.3g

- Carbohydrates: 11.2g

- Fiber: 0.5g

- Sodium: 531mg

- Protein: 27.2g

2. Egg & & Cheese Puffs

Preparation Time: 15 mins Cooking Time: 20 mins

Servings: 4

Ingredients:

- 1 (8-ounce) frozen puff pastry sheet, thawed

- ¾ cup Monterey Jack cheese, shredded and divided

- 4 large eggs 1 tablespoon fresh chives, minced

Directions:

1. Unfold the puff pastry and arrange onto a lightly floured surface. Cut pastry into 4 equal-sized squares.

2. Arrange 2 squares onto the sheet pan.

3. Press "Power" button of Ninja Foodi Digital Air Fry Oven and turn the dial to select "Air Fry" mode.

4. Press "Time" button and again turn the dial to set the cooking time to 10 minutes. Now push "Temp" button and rotate the dial to set the temperature at 390 degrees F.

5. Press "Start/Pause" button to start.

6. When the unit beeps to show that it is preheated, open the lid.

7. Insert the sheet pan in the oven.

8. After 5 minutes, press "Start/Pause" button to pause.

9. Remove the sheet pan of pastry from the oven.

10. With a metal spoon, press down the center of each pastry to make a nest.

11. Place ¼ of the cheese into each nest and carefully, push it to the sides.

12. Carefully crack an egg into each nest and again insert the sheet pan in the oven.

13. Press "Start/Pause" button to start.

14. When the unit beeps to show that cooking time is completed, press "Power" button to stop cooking and open the lid.

15. Transfer the puffs onto serving plates.

16. Repeat with the remaining pastry squares, cheese and eggs.

17. Garnish with chives and serve warm.

Nutrition:

- Calories: 98 Fat: 27.6g

- Saturated Fat 7.6g Trans Fat: 20g

- Carbohydrates: 26.2g Fiber: 0.6g

- Sodium: 234mg Protein: 11.3g

3. Honey-Lime Glazed Grilled Fruit Salad

Preparation time: 10 minutes

Cooking time: 4 minutes

Servings: 4

Ingredients:

- 1/2 lb. (227 g.) strawberries, washed, hulled, and halved

- 1 (9 oz./255 g.) can pineapple chunks, drained, juice reserved

- 2 peaches, pitted and sliced

- 6 tbsp. honey, divided

- 1 tbsp. freshly lime juice, squeezed

Directions:

1. Pull-out the Grill Grate and close the covering. Select GRILL, fixed the temperature to MAX, and fixed the time to 4 minutes. Select START/STOP to preheat.

2. While the unit is preheating, combine the strawberries, pineapple, and peaches in a large bowl with 3 tbsp. of honey. Throw to coat evenly.

3. When the unit honks to indicate it has preheated, place the fruit on the Grill Grate. Gently press the fruit down to

maximize grill marks. Close the hood and GRILL for 4 minutes without flipping.

4. Meanwhile, in a small bowl, combine the remaining 3 tbsp. of honey, lime juice, and 1 tbsp. of reserved pineapple juice.

5. When cooking is complete, place the fruit in a large bowl and toss it with the honey mixture? Serve immediately.

Nutrition:

- Calories: 240

- Fat: 4 g.

- Saturated Fat: 1 g.

- Carbohydrates: 43 g.

- Fiber: 8 g.

- Sodium: 85 mg.

- Protein: 2 g.

4. Awesome Tater Tots Eggs

Preparation time: 10 minutes.

Cooking time: 25 minutes.

Servings: 4

Ingredients:

- 1 pound frozen tater tots

- 1 cup Cheddar cheese, shredded

- 2 sausages, cooked and sliced

- Cooking spray as needed

- Salt and pepper to taste

- ¼ cup milk

- 5 whole eggs

Directions:

- Preheat your Ninja Foodi Smart XL in Bake mode at 390°F for 3 minutes.

- Take a bowl and add eggs, milk, season with salt and pepper.

- Take a small baking pan and grease it with oil.

- Add egg mix to the pan and transfer to your Ninja Food Smart XL.

- Cook for 5 minutes, place sausages on top of eggs, sprinkle cheese on top.

- Bake for 20 minutes more.

- Serve and enjoy!

Nutrition:

- **Calories:** 187

- **Fat:** 8 g

- **Saturated Fat:** 3 g

- **Carbohydrates:** 21 g

- **Fibre:** 1 g

- **Sodium:** 338 mg

- **Protein:** 9 g

5. Smoky Red Bean and Bacon Wraps

Preparation time: 30 minutes.

Cooking time: 40 minutes.

Servings: 4

Ingredients:

For the rice:

- 1 teaspoon olive oil

- ¼ cup minced onion

- ¾ cup basmati rice

- 1(½) cups chicken broth

For the beans:

- 4 thick bacon slices, cut into 1-inch-wide pieces

- 1 cup diced onions (½-inch dice)

- 4 celery stalks, cut into ¼-inch pieces

- 1 garlic clove, minced

- 1 medium bell pepper, cut into ½-inch dice

- 1(15-ounce) can small red beans, rinsed and drained

- ¼ teaspoon smoked paprika

- ¼ teaspoon freshly ground black pepper

- 1/8 teaspoon cayenne pepper

- ½ cup water

- 2 tablespoons minced fresh flat-leaf parsley

Directions:

To make the rice:

1. Preheat the Ninja Foodi Smart XL Grill to 350°F. Heat the oil and add the onion and sauté briefly, 1 to 2 minutes, until the onion is soft. Put the rice and cook, stirring, for 3 to 4 minutes until the rice starts to turn opaque and has some golden colour.

2. Transfer the mixture to a 9-inch square glass baking dish and pour the broth over the rice. Stir to mix in the broth, cover the dish with aluminum foil, and bake for 30 minutes. Remove the dish from the oven and set it aside.

To make the beans:

3. While the rice is baking, wipe your skillet and place it over Medium-high heat. Cook the bacon for 7 to 9 minutes, occasionally stirring, until the bacon is crispy and the fat is rendered. Remove the bacon with a spoon and transfer it to

a paper towel-lined plate to drain. Use more paper towels to press as much fat out of the bacon as possible.

4. Set the Ninja Foodi Smart to Medium heat, leaving 2 teaspoons of bacon fat in the skillet. Add the onions and celery and then cook for 2 to 3 minutes until the vegetables start to soften.

5. Lower the heat to standard and add the beans, paprika, pepper, and cayenne to the skillet. Stir to mix and add ½ cup of water. Simmer the beans gently for 15 to 20 minutes until the liquid has reduced and thickened, and the beans are soft when mashed with a spoon. If necessary, add another ¼ cup of water to the mix to keep it simmering.

6. **To dehydrate:** Spread the bean mix out evenly on the dehydrator trays fitted with a solid plastic insert, ensuring that any liquid in the mix is included on the trays. Spread the rice out on separate trays.

7. At the 7-hour mark, check the vegetables and rice. The vegetables should be firm and should not feel moist. If necessary, continue to dry them for another 1 to 2 hours.

Keep in mind that rice will dry more quickly than vegetables, so remove the rice when it is dry and hard to the touch.

8. **To store:** Measure the total amount of beans and rice separately. Divide both the beans and rice into four portions and place one portion of each into four boil-in bags. Label and date the bags. Store for up to 6 months.

9. **To rehydrate:** Add ¾ cup of boiling water to the bag. Mix it well, cover, and let sit for about 15 minutes. Stir the rice and beans again and wrap them into a tortilla, if using, before eating.

Nutrition:

- **Calories:** 590
- **Fat:** 19g
- **Carb:** 80g
- **Protein:** 20g
- **Sodium:** 1130mg

CHAPTER 3:

Meat Recipes

6. Lamb Ribs with Fresh Mint

Preparation time: 5 minutes

Cooking time: 18 minutes

Servings: 4

Ingredients:

- 2 tablespoons mustard

- 1-pound (454 g) lamb ribs

- 1 teaspoon rosemary, chopped

- Salt and ground black pepper, to taste

- ¼ cup mint leaves, chopped

- 1 cup Greek yogurt

Direction

1. Pull-out the Crisper Basket and adjust the hood. Choose AIR CRISP set the temperature to 350°F (177°C) and set the time to 18 minutes. Select START/STOP to begin preheating.

2. Use a brush to spread over the mustard to the lamb ribs, and flavor with rosemary, salt, and pepper. Handover to the basket.

3. Close the hood and AIR CRISP for 18 min.

4. Temporarily, add the mint leaves and yogurt in a bowl.

5. Eliminate the lamb ribs from the grill when prepared and serve with the mint yogurt.

Nutrition:

- Calories: 170

- Fat: 5 g

- Carb: 13 g

Proteins: 16 g

7. Juicy Steak and Pineapple

Preparation time: 10 minutes

Cooking time: 8 minutes

Servings: 4

Ingredients:

- 1/2 medium pineapple, cored and diced

- 1 jalapeno, seeded and stemmed, diced

- 1 medium red onion, diced

- 4 (6–8 oz. each) filet mignon steaks

- 1 tbsp. canola oil

- Salt and pepper to taste

- 1 tbsp. lime juice

- 1/4 cup cilantro leaves, chopped

- ¼ tbs. Chili powder

- ¼ tbs. ground coriander

Directions:

1. Rub fillets with oil evenly, season them well with salt and pepper.

2. Pre-heat Ninja Foodi by demanding the GRILL option and situation it to HIGH and timer to 8 minutes.

3. Let it pre-heat till you hear a beep.

4. Arrange fillets over grill grate, lock the lid and cook for 4 minutes until the internal temperature reaches 125°F.

5. Take a mixing bowl and add pineapple, onion, jalapeno, and mix well.

6. Add lime juice, cilantro, chili powder, coriander and combine.

7. Serve fillets with the pineapple mixture on top.

8. Enjoy!

Nutrition:

- Calories: 530

- Carbohydrates: 21 g.

- Fat: 22 g.

- Protein: 58 g.

8. Spicy T-Bone Steak with Aromatics

Preparation time: 20 minutes.

Cooking time: 15 minutes.

Servings: 3

Ingredients:

- 1 pound T-Bone steak

- 4 garlic cloves, halved

- 2 tablespoons olive oil

- 1/4 cup tamari sauce

- 4 tablespoons tomato paste

- 1 teaspoon sriracha sauce

- 2 tablespoons white vinegar

- 1 teaspoon dried rosemary

- 1/2 teaspoon dried basil

- 2 heaping tablespoons cilantro, chopped

Directions:

- Rub the garlic halves all over the T-bone steak.

- Drizzle the oil all over the steak, transfer it to the grill pan; broil the steak in the preheated Ninja Foodi Smart at 400°F for 10 minutes.

- Meanwhile, whisk the tamari sauce, tomato paste, Sriracha, vinegar, rosemary, and basil. Cook an additional 5 minutes.

- Serve garnished with fresh cilantro.

Nutrition:

- **Calories:** 428

- **Fat:** 24.6g

- **Carbs:** 7.1g

- **Protein:** 43.7g

- **Fibre:** 1.5g

9. BBQ Skirt Steak

Preparation time: 20 minutes + marinating time.

Cooking time: 15 minutes.

Servings: 5

Ingredients:

- 2 pounds skirt steak

- 2 tablespoons tomato paste

- 1 tablespoon olive oil

- 1 tablespoon coconut aminos

- 1/4 cup rice vinegar

- 1 tablespoon fish sauce

- Sea salt to taste

- 1/2 teaspoon dried dill

- 1/2 teaspoon dried rosemary

- 1/4 teaspoon black pepper, freshly cracked

Directions:

- Place all the ingredients in a large ceramic dish; let it marinate for 3 hours in your refrigerator.

- Spray the cooking basket with the cooking spray.

- Add your steak to the cooking basket; reserve the marinade. Select 'broil' mode and cook the skirt steak in the preheated Ninja Foodi Smart XL Grill at 400°F. Select 12 minutes, turning over a couple of times, basting with the reserved marinade.

Nutrition:

- **Calories:** 401

- **Fat:** 21g

- **Carbs:** 1.7g

- **Protein:** 51g

- **Fibre:** 1g

10. Beer Beef

Preparation Time: 15 minutes

Cooking Time: 7 hours

Servings: 8 - 12

Ingredients:

- 1 beef brisket 9 - 12 lbs. the fat outside trimmed

- 5 garlic cloves, smashed

- 1 onion, sliced

- 5 tbsp. of pickling spice

- 1 tbsp. of curing salt for each lb. of meat

- ½ cup of brown sugar

- 1 ½ cups salt

- 3x12 oz. dark beer

- 3 quarts water, cold

- Rib seasoning

Directions:

1. In a stockpot, combine the curing salt, brown sugar, salt, beer, and water. Stir until well dissolved.

2. Add the garlic, onion, and pickling spice — place in the fridge.

3. Add the meat to the brine but make sure that it is submerged completely. Brine for 2 - 4 days. Stir once every day.

4. Rinse the brisket under cold water. Sprinkle with rib seasoning.

5. Preheat the grill to 250 °F.

6. Cook the brisket for about 4 to 5 hours. The inside temperature should be 160 °F.

7. Wrap the meat in a foil (double layer) and add water (1 ½ cup). Put it back on the grill and let it cook for 3 to 4 hours until it reaches 204 °F internal temperature.

8. Set aside and let it sit for 30 min. Crave into thin pieces and serve. Enjoy!

Nutrition:

- Calories: 320

- Proteins: 38 g

- Carbs: 14 g

- Fat: 12 g

11. Honey-Glazed Pork Tenderloin

Preparation Time: 10 minutes

Cooking Time: 20 minutes

Servings: 4

Ingredients:

- 1 tbsp. soy sauce

- ½ tsp. garlic powder ½ tsp. sea salt

- 1 (1½-pound) pork tenderloin

- 2 tbsp. Honey

Directions:

1. Put inside the grill grate and close the hood. Select Grill, set the temperature to Medium, and set the time to 20 minutes. Select Start/stop to begin preheating.

2. In the meantime, in a small bowl, combine the honey, soy sauce, garlic powder, and salt.

3. When the Ninja Foodi smart XL beeps, it has preheated, then place the pork tenderloin on the grill grate. Baste all sides with the honey glaze. Close the hood and cook for 8 minutes. After 8 minutes, flip the pork tenderloin and baste with any

remaining glaze. Close the hood and cook for 7 minutes more.

4. It is completely cooked when the internal temperature of the pork reaches 145 °F. on a food thermometer. If needed, cook for up to 5 minutes more.

5. Remove the pork, and set it on a cutting board to rest for 5 minutes. Slice and serve.

Nutrition:

- Calories: 589

- Protein: 18.21 g

- Fat: 49.63 g

- Carbohydrates: 17.5 g

12.   Charred Korean-Style Steak Tips

Preparation Time: 35 minutes

Cooking Time: 13 minutes

Servings: 4

Ingredients:

- 4 garlic cloves, minced

- ½ apple, peeled and grated

- 3 tbsp. Sesame oil

- 3 tbsp. brown sugar

- 1/3 cup of soy sauce

- 1 tsp. freshly ground black pepper Sea salt

- 1½ pounds beef tips

Directions:

1. In a prepared medium bowl, combine the garlic, apple, sesame oil, sugar, soy sauce, pepper, and salt until well mixed.

2. Place the beef tips in a large shallow bowl and pour the marinade over them. Cover and refrigerate for 30 minutes.

3. Place inside the grill grate and close the hood. Select Grill, set the temperature to Medium, and set the time to 13 minutes. Select Start/stop to begin preheating.

4. When the Ninja Foodi Smart XL beeps, it has preheated, then place the steak tips on the grill grate. Close the hood and cook for 11 minutes.

5. Cooking is completed to Medium doneness when the meat's internal temperature reaches 145 °F. on a food thermometer. If desired, cook for up to 2 minutes more.

6. Remove the steak, and set it on a cutting board to rest for 5 minutes. Serve.

Nutrition:

- Calories: 417

- Protein: 38.17 g

- Fat: 21.99 g

- Carbohydrates: 15.35 g

13.   Kalbi Short Ribs

Preparation time: 20 minutes.

Cooking time: 2 hours and 30 minutes. **Servings: 4**

Ingredients:

- 1.10 pound Crosscut beef short ribs

Marinade:

- 2 tablespoons sesame oil 2 tablespoons brown sugar

- 1(½) teaspoon chili flakes 1 tablespoon chopped garlic

- ½ cup soy sauce ¼ cup chopped green onions

- ¼ cup orange juice

Directions:

- Heat the Ninja Foodi smart pan on medium-high heat and add in the sesame oil and garlic. Let the garlic cook for 2 minutes, then take the pan off the heat. Add the rest of the marinade ingredients to the pan while it's still warm and stir the mixture until well combined.

- Put the ribs in a baking dish and pour in the marinade. Place the dish in the refrigerator, covered for 1 hour. Turn the meat every 15 minutes.

- Preheat your Ninja Foodi Smart to 138°F or 59°C

- Roast the beef short ribs until it reaches 145°F.

- While the meat is cooking, put the marinade in a pot and allow it to come to a boil. Let the sauce cook for 15 to 20 minutes until it starts to reduce a little.

- When the steaks are cooked, use a brush to coat them with the marinade.

- Place the ribs on an aluminum foil-lined rimmed baking sheet or pan.

- Put the baking sheet on the Ninja broiling pan and let the meat cook for 1 to 2 minutes per side. You just want the sauce to caramelize.

- Serve the ribs immediately.

Nutrition:

- **Energy (calories):** 356 **rotein:** 14.09g

- **Fat:** 19.88g **Carbohydrates:** 30.88g

14.   Marinated Pork Belly

Preparation time: 5 minutes.

Cooking time: 8 hours.

Servings: 4

Ingredients:

- 1 pound pork belly

- 1/4 cup soy sauce

- 1/4 cup mirin or 1/4 cup white wine

- 1 tablespoon sugar

- 1/4 cup sugar

Directions:

- Preheat your sous vide to 170°F or 76.7°C.

- Place all the ingredients in the bag you're going to use to sous vide and seal the bag.

- Place the bag in the preheated water and Set the timer for 8 hours.

- When the pork belly is almost done, preheat your broiler Ninja Foodi Smart XL.

- Place the marinade from the bag into a saucepan and cut the pork belly into ¼ thick pieces.

- Put a baking sheet or broiler pan with aluminum foil and place the pork belly on it.

- Place the baking sheet or pan under the broiler and cook for 3 to 5 minutes. The pork belly should be crispy when done.

- Bring the marinade liquid to a boil on high heat then, lower the temperature to medium-low to simmer. Lessen the sauce and allow it to thicken.

- Pour the sauce reduced sauce over the pork belly to serve.

Nutrition:

- **Energy (calories):** 673

- **Protein:** 12.05g

- **Fat:** 63.04g

- **Carbohydrates:** 13.89g

15.   Spicy Roast Goat

Preparation time: 30 minutes.**ooking:** 1 hour. **Servings:** 5

Ingredients:

- 1 cup of onion, chopped

- 2 green onions, chopped

- 1 teaspoon ginger, minced

- 2 large tomatoes, chopped

- 2–1/2 pounds goat meat, cubed

- 3 cups or more water

- 1–1/2 tablespoons beef or chicken bouillon powder

- 3 tablespoons cooking oil

- 1 teaspoon smoked paprika 1/2 teaspoon curry powder

- 1 red or green bell pepper, chopped

- 2 or more scotch bonnet pepper

- 2 teaspoons garlic, minced Salt and white pepper to taste

Directions:

- In a baking of Ninja Foodi smart, mix goat, water, 1/2 tablespoon of bouillon powder, salt, pepper, and some chopped onions.

- Select the bake and set the temperature to 400°F.

- Cook the goat meat until tender for 1 hour.

- With a slotted spoon, transfer goat meat to a baking tray lined with foil.

- Select the broil function.

- Broil goat for 10 minutes, turning halfway until brown. Set aside.

- Add some cooking oil to the tray.

- Add the remaining chopped onion, ginger, and garlic.

- After 1 minute, add green onion, paprika, curry powder, tomatoes, scotch bonnet, white pepper, and 1 tablespoon bouillon powder.

- Cook for 7 minutes.

- Add broiled goat and bell peppers and cook for 3 more minutes, stirring occasionally.

Nutrition:

- **Energy (calories):** 236 **Protein:** 27.33g

- **Fat:** 10.06g **Carbohydrates:** 9.02g

16.   Tomato Sauce with Ground Goat

Preparation time: 18 minutes.

Cooking time: 1 hour.

Servings: 20

Ingredients:

- 4 garlic cloves

- 1 large onion, diced

- 8 ounces can chipotle peppers in adobo, pureed

- 2 medium red vine tomatoes, diced

- 1-ounces cilantro, chopped

- 2 jalapenos, diced

- 4 pounds ground goat meat

- 1 ounces grapeseed oil

Directions:

- Choose the air fry option. Coat pot with oil.

- Air fry 1/3 of the onions until soft and brown for 350°F for 6 minutes.

- Add garlic and cook for 1 minute, then add meat and cook for 3 minutes, stirring occasionally.

- Add half the chipotle pepper, tomatoes, and jalapeno. Then add water just enough to submerge meat.

- Select the bake function. Bake at 300°F for 45 minutes to 1 hour.

- In a baking tray lay the remaining tomatoes evenly.

- Broil for 3 minutes or until blackened. Do not move tomatoes until they begin to caramelize.

- Divide blackened tomatoes into two. Dice half and use for garnish. Puree half and use it as a sauce.

Nutrition:

- Energy (calories): 164

- Protein: 20.63g

- Fat: 7.04g

- Carbohydrates: 4.13g

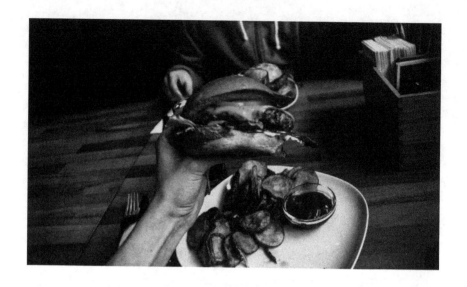

CHAPTER 4:

Fish Recipes

17.   Fish and Chips

Preparation time: 20 min

Cooking time: 39 min

Servings: 4

Ingredients:

- 2 eggs

- 8 ounces ale beer 1 cup cornstarch

- 1 cup all-purpose flour ½ tablespoon chili powder

- 1 tablespoon ground cumin

- 1 teaspoon sea salt

- 1 teaspoon black pepper

- 4 (5- to 6-ounce) cod fillets

- Nonstick cooking spray

- 2 russet potatoes, cut into ¼- to ½-inch matchsticks

- 2 tablespoons vegetable oil

Directions:

1. Place the Cook & Crisp Basket in the pot and adjust the Crisping Lid. Warm the unit by selecting Air Crisp, adjust the temperature to 375°F, and setting the time to 5 minutes.

2. In the meantime, in a shallow mixing bowl, whisk together the eggs and beer. In a detached medium bowl, whip together the cornstarch, flour, chili powder, cumin, salt, and pepper.

3. Coat each cod fillet in the egg mixture, then dredge in the flour mixture, the coating on all sides.

4. Spray the preheated Cook & Crisp Basket with nonstick cooking spray. Place the fish fillets in the basket and coat them with cooking spray.

5. Close the Crisping Lid. Select Air Crisp, set the temperature to 375°F and set the time to 15 minutes. Press Start/Stop to begin.

6. Meanwhile, toss the potatoes with the oil and season with salt and pepper.

7. After 15 minutes, check the fish for your desired crispiness. Remove the fish from the basket.

8. Place the potatoes in the Cook & Crisp™ Basket. Adjust the Crisping Lid. Choose Air Crisp set the temperature to 400°F and set the time to 24 minutes. Press Start/Stop to begin.

9. After 12 minutes, open the lid, then lift the basket and shake the fries. Lesser the basket back into the pot and adjust the lid to resume cooking until they reach your desired crispiness.

TIP: I love using this technique to replicate a deep-fried beer batter. It is as great a technique to use for chicken fingers and nuggets as it is for fish.

Nutrition:

- Calories: 674 Total fat: 11 g

- Saturated fat: 2 g

- Cholesterol: 166 mg

- Sodium: 1299 mg

- Carbohydrates: 100 g

- Fiber: 3 g Protein: 35 g

18.   Mahi and Salsa

Preparation: 15 minutes **Cooking:** 12 minutes **Servings:** 4

Ingredients:

- 4 Mahi fillets   tbsp. vegetable oil Salt and pepper to taste

For basting:

- 1/4 cup honey 3 tbsp. lime juice 2 tbsp. creole seasoning

- 1 tbsp. cilantro, chopped

For salsa:

- 1 tsp. cumin

- 1/4 cup lime juice

- 1 tbsp. cilantro, chopped

- 1 cup pineapple chunks

- 1 red bell pepper, chopped

- 1 onion, chopped

- 1 jalapeño pepper, chopped

Directions:

1. Coat fish with oil.

2. Season with salt and pepper.

3. In a bowl, mix basting ingredients.

4. Set your unit to GRILL.

5. Set temperature to max and time to 15 minutes.

6. Press START.

7. After the unit beeps, add fish to the grill.

8. Brush the top with the basting sauce.

9. Cook for 6 minutes.

10. Offhand and brush the other side with the sauce.

11. Cook for another 6 minutes.

12. In another bowl, mix the salsa ingredients.

13. Serve fish with salsa.

14. Serving Suggestions: Garnish with cucumber and tomato slices.

15. Preparation & Cooking Tips: You can also grill pineapple rings and slice to be used for the salsa.

Nutrition:

- Calories: 250 Fat: 8 g. Saturated Fat: 3 g.

- Carbohydrates: 22 g. Fiber: 3 g. Sodium: 370 mg.

- Protein: 36 g.

CHAPTER 5:

Vegetable Recipes

19.   Mushroom and Gruyere Tarts

Preparation time: 15 minutes

Cooking time: 31 minutes

Servings: 4

Ingredients:

- 2 tablespoons extra-virgin olive oil, divided

- 1 small white onion, sliced

- 5 ounces shiitake mushrooms, sliced

- ¼ teaspoon of sea salt

- ¼ teaspoon freshly ground black pepper

- ¼ cup dry white wine

- 1 sheet puff pastry, thawed

- 1 cup shredded Gruyere cheese

- 1 tablespoon thinly sliced fresh chives

Directions:

1. Select Sear/Sauté. Set it to High. Press Start/Stop to begin and preheat for 5 minutes.

2. Combine 1 tablespoon of oil, the onion, and the mushrooms in the pot. Cook, occasionally stirring, for 5 minutes, or until

the vegetables are browned and tender. Season with salt and black pepper, then add the wine and cook until it has evaporated about 2 minutes. Place the vegetables in a bowl and set aside.

3. Unfold the puff pastry and then cut it into 4 squares. Using a fork, pierce the dough and brush both sides with the remaining 1 tablespoon of oil.

4. Evenly divide half the cheese among the puff pastry squares, leaving a ½-inch border around the edges. Divide the mushroom and onion mixture among the pastry squares, then divide the remaining cheese among them.

5. Place the Cook & Crisp Basket in the pot. Close the Crisping Lid. Preheat the unit by selecting Air Crisp, setting the temperature to 400°F, and setting the time to 5 minutes.

6. Once preheated, place 1 tart in the Cook & Crisp™ Basket.

7. Close the Crisping Lid. Select Air Crisp, set it to 360°F and set the time to 6 minutes. Select Start/Stop to begin.

8. After 6 minutes, check for your desired browning. Remove the tart from the basket and transfer to a plate.

9. Repeat steps 6 through 8 with the remaining tarts.

10. Serve garnished with chives

TIP: These tarts make for a tasty appetizer or a light meal. When served as a main, pair them with a mixed green salad dressed with mustard vinaigrette.

Nutrition:

- Calories: 550

- Total fat: 39 g

- Saturated fat: 12 g

- Cholesterol: 30 mg

- Sodium: 394 mg

- Carbohydrates: 34 g

- Fiber: 2 g; Protein: 15 g.

- Calories: 200

- Fat: 12 g

- Carb: 16 g

- Proteins: 15 g

20. Mexican Corn Dish

Preparation time: 5–10 minutes

Cooking time: 12 minutes

Servings: 4

Ingredients:

- 2 tbsp. lime juice

- 1/2 cup mayonnaise

- 1/2 cup sour cream

- 2 tsp. garlic powder

- 2 tsp. onion powder

- 1 1/4 cups Cotija cheese, crumbled

- Salt and pepper to taste

- 3 tbsp. canola oil

- 6 ears corn

Directions:

1. Set your Ninja Foodi Smart XL to GRILL mode, set the temperature to MAX, and timer to 12 minutes.

2. Let it preheat until you hear a beep.

3. Brush the corn ears with oil, season with salt and pepper.

4. Transfer to grill and cook for 6 minutes per side.

5. Take a bowl and mix in the remaining ingredients; mix well.

6. Cover corn mix and serve.

7. Enjoy!

Nutrition:

- Calories: 156

- Fat: 10 g.

- Saturated Fat: 3 g.

- Carbohydrates: 15 g.

- Fiber: 3 g.

- Sodium: 163 mg.

- Protein: 6 g.

21.   Baked Broccoli Cauliflower

Preparation time: 10 minutes.

Cooking time: 30 minutes.

Servings: 6

Ingredients:

- 4 cups cauliflower florets

- 4 cups broccoli florets

- 2/3 cup Parmesan cheese, shredded

- 4 garlic cloves, minced

- 1/3 cup olive oil

- Pepper to taste

- Salt to taste

Directions:

- Add half Parmesan cheese, broccoli, cauliflower, garlic, oil, pepper, and salt into the large bowl and toss well.

- Place the cooking pot in the Ninja Foodi Smart XL, then close the hood.

- Select bake mode and then set the temperature to 390°F and set the timer to 20 minutes. Press start to begin preheating.

- Once the unit is preheated, one beep sounds, then place cauliflower broccoli mixture in the cooking pot. Close the hood.

- Cook for 20 minutes.

- Add the remaining cheese.

- Toss well and serve.

Nutrition:

- Calories: 165

- Fat: 13.6g

- Carbohydrates: 8.6g

- Sugar: 3g

- Protein: 6.4g

- Cholesterol: 7mg

CHAPTER 6:

Appetizers and Snacks Recipes

22. Kale Salad Sushi Rolls with Sriracha Mayonnaise

Preparation time: 10 minutes

Cooking time: 10 minutes

Servings: 12

Ingredients:

Kale Salad:

- 1½ cups chopped kale
- 1 tablespoon sesame seeds
- ¾ teaspoon soy sauce
- ¾ teaspoon toasted sesame oil
- ½ teaspoon rice vinegar
- ¼ teaspoon ginger
- 1/8 teaspoon garlic powder

Sushi rolls:

- 3 sheets sushi nori
- 1 batch cauliflower rice
- ½ avocado, sliced

- Sriracha Mayonnaise:

- ¼ cup Sriracha sauce

- ¼ cup vegan mayonnaise

Coating:

- ½ cup panko breadcrumbs

Directions:

1. Insert the Crisper Basket and close the hood. Select AIR CRISP, set the temperature to 390°F (199°C), and set the time to 10 minutes. Select START/STOP to preheat.

2. In a medium bowl, toss all the ingredients for the salad together until well coated and set aside.

3. Place a sheet of nori on a clean work surface and spread the cauliflower rice in an even layer on the nori. Scoop 2 to 3 tablespoon of kale salad on the rice and spread over. Place 1 or 2 avocado slices on top. Roll up the sushi, pressing gently to get a nice, tight roll. Repeat to make the remaining 2 rolls.

4. In a bowl, stir together the Sriracha sauce and mayonnaise until smooth. Add breadcrumbs to a separate bowl.

5. Dredge the sushi rolls in Sriracha Mayonnaise, then roll in breadcrumbs till well coated.

6. Place the coated sushi rolls in the Crisper Basket. Close the hood and AIR CRISP for 10 minutes, or until golden brown and crispy. Flip the sushi rolls gently halfway through to ensure even cooking...

7. Transfer to a platter and rest for 5 minutes before slicing each roll into 8 pieces. Serve warm.

Nutrition:

- Calories: 327
- Fat: 5 g
- Saturated Fat: 0.5 g
- Carbohydrates: 328 g
- Fiber: 2 g
- Sodium: 524 mg
- Protein: 8 g

23. Lamb and Feta Hamburgers

Preparation time: 15 minutes

Cooking time: 16 minutes

Servings: 4 burgers

Ingredients:

- 1½ pounds (680 g) ground lamb

- ¼ cup crumbled feta

- 1½ teaspoons tomato paste

- 1½ teaspoons minced garlic

- 1 teaspoon ground dried ginger

- 1 teaspoon ground coriander

- ¼ teaspoon salt

- ¼ teaspoon cayenne pepper

- 4 Kaiser rolls or hamburger buns, split open lengthwise, warmed

- Cooking spray

Directions:

1. Spritz the Crisper Basket with cooking spray.

2. Insert the Crisper Basket and close the hood. Select AIR CRISP, set the temperature to 375°F (191°C), and set the time to 16 minutes. Select START/STOP to begin preheating.

3. Combine all the ingredients, except for the buns, in a large bowl. Coarsely stir to mix well.

4. Shape the mixture into four balls, then pound the balls into four 5-inch diameter patties.

5. Arrange the patties in the basket and spritz with cooking spray. Close the hood and AIR CRISP for 16 minutes or until well browned. Flip the patties halfway through.

6. Assemble the buns with patties to make the burgers and serve immediately.

Nutrition:

- Calories: 240
- Carbs: 31 g
- Fat: 15 g
- Protein: 7 g

24.   Mustard Veggie Mix

Preparation time: 5–10 minutes

Cooking time: 30-40 minutes

Servings: 4

Ingredients:

For vinaigrette:

- 1/2 cup olive oil

- 1/2 cup avocado oil

- 1/4 tsp. pepper

- 1 tsp. salt

- 2 tbsp. honey

- 1/2 cup red wine vinegar

- 2 tbsp. Dijon mustard

For veggies:

- 4 zucchinis, halved

- 4 sweet onion, quartered

- 4 red pepper, seeded and halved

- 2 bunch green onions, trimmed

- 4 yellow squash, cut in half

Directions:

1. Take a small bowl and whisk in mustard, honey, vinegar, salt, and pepper. Add oil and mix well.

2. Set your Ninja Foodi Smart XL to GRILL mode and MED setting, set timer to 10 minutes.

3. Transfer onion quarter to Grill Grate, cook for 5 minutes.

4. Flip and cook for 5 minutes more.

5. Grill remaining veggies in the same way, giving 7 minutes per side for zucchini and 1 minute for green onions.

6. Serve with mustard vinaigrette on top.

7. Enjoy!

Nutrition:

- Calories: 334 Fat: 4.5 g.

- Saturated Fat: 0.6 g.

- Carbohydrates: 345 g.

- Fiber: 1.5 g.

- Sodium: 456 mg.

- Protein: 7.8 g.

25. Outstanding Magical 5 Ingredient Shrimp

Preparation: 10 minutes **Cooking** 15 minutes **Servings:** 4 sliders

Ingredients:

- 2 tbsp. butter 1/2 tsp. smoked paprika

- 1 lb. shrimps, peeled and deveined

- Lemongrass stalks 1 red chili pepper, seeded and chopped

Directions:

1. Take a bowl and mix all the ingredients well, except lemongrass and marinate for 1 hour.

2. Transfer to Ninja Foodi and lock lid, BAKE/ROAST for 15 minutes at 345°F.

3. Once done, serve and enjoy!

Nutrition:

- Calories: 225 Fat: 17 g.

- Saturated Fat: 5 g. Carbohydrates: 13 g.

- Fiber: 3 g. Sodium: 284 mg.Protein: 6 g.

26.   Herbed Pita Chips

Preparation time: 5 minutes.

Cooking time: 5–6 minutes.

Servings: 4

Ingredients:

- ¼ teaspoon dried basil

- ¼ teaspoon marjoram

- ¼ teaspoon ground oregano

- ¼ teaspoon garlic powder

- ¼ teaspoon ground thyme

- ¼ teaspoon salt

- 2 whole 6-inch pitas, whole grain or white

- Cooking spray

Directions:

- Insert the Crisper Basket and close the hood. Select bake, set the temperature to 330°F (166°C) and set the time to 6 minutes. Select start/stop to begin preheating.

- Mix all the seasonings.

- Cut each pita half into four wedges. Break apart wedges at the fold.

- Spray one side of pita wedges with oil and then add half of the seasoning mix.

- Turn pita wedges over,spray the other side with oil and then add the remaining seasonings.

- Place pita wedges in Crisper Basket. Close the hood and bake for 2 minutes.

- Shake the basket and bake for 2 minutes longer. Shake again, and if needed, bake for 1 or 2 more minutes, or until crisp. Observe because, at this point, they will cook very quickly.

- Serve hot.

Nutrition:

- **Energy (calories):** 485

- **Protein:** 17.9g

- **Fat:** 4.74g

- **Carbohydrates:** 100.36g

27.   Enchiladas

Preparation time: 10 minutes.

Cooking time: 30 minutes.

Servings: 16

Ingredients:

- 16 tortillas

- 5 pounds Mexican chicken, shredded

- 3 cups enchilada sauce

- 3 pounds Mexican shredded cheese

Directions:

- Spray the tortillas with cooking spray and arrange 6 of them in the air fryer basket of the Ninja Foodi. Make sure they overlap as little as possible.

- Select "air fry" at 425ªF with a 4-minute timer.

- Repeat until all of your tortillas are pliable.

- Put 2–3 tablespoons of the shredded chicken in each tortilla and wrap.

- Arrange enchiladas in the baking dish and pour 2.5 tablespoons of the sauce over each enchilada.

- Put the baking dish in the Ninja Foodi Smart XL Grill and select "bake" at 325ªF with a timer of 20 minutes.

- When done, sprinkle with the cheese and return to the oven.

- Select "broil" at 510ªF for 2 minutes.

- Serve and enjoy!

Nutrition:

- **Calories:** 614

- **Fat:** 30.9g

- **Carbohydrates:** 29g

- **Fiber:** 2g

- **Sodium:** 1071mg

- **Protein:** 53g

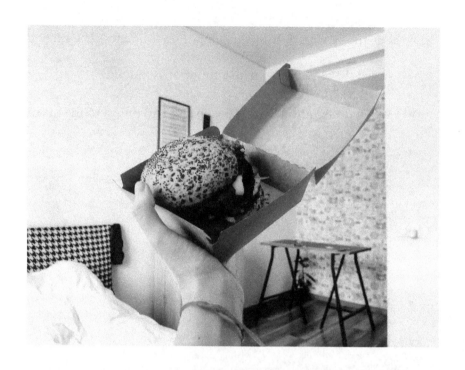

CHAPTER 7:

Desserts Recipes

28. Peanut Butter and Chocolate Lava Cakes

Preparation time: 15 minutes

Cooking time: 20 minutes

Servings: 4

Ingredients:

- Nonstick cooking spray

- 8 tbsp. (1 stick) unsalted butter

- 1/4 cup dark chocolate chips

- 1/4 cup peanut butter chips

- 2 eggs

- 3 egg yolks

- 1 1/4 cups confectioners' sugar

- 1 tsp. vanilla extract 1/2 cup all-purpose flour

Directions:

- Preheat the unit by choosing BAKE/ROAST, set the temperature to 300°F and setting the time to 5 minutes. Press START/STOP to begin.

- Meanwhile, grease 4 ramekins with cooking spray and set them aside.

- In a microwave-safe medium bowl, combine the butter, chocolate chips, and peanut butter chips. Microwave on high until melted, checking and stirring every 15–20 seconds.

- Add the eggs, egg yolks, confectioners' sugar, and vanilla to the chocolate mixture and whisk until smooth. Mingling in the flour a little at a time until combined and incorporated.

- Divide the batter among the ramekins and wrap each with aluminum foil. Place the ramekins on the Reversible Rack, making sure the rack is in the lower position. Place the rack in the pot.

- Close the Crisping Lid. Select BAKE/ROAST, set the temperature to 300°F, and set the time to 20 minutes. Select START/STOP to begin.

- When cooking is complete, remove the rack from the pot. Remove the foil and allow the ramekins to cool for 1–2 minutes.

- Reverse the lava cakes onto a plate and serve immediately.

Tip: Take these cakes one step further and serve with a scoop of vanilla ice cream on the side.

Nutrition:

- Calories: 587

- Total fat: 37 g.

- Saturated fat: 21 g.

- Cholesterol: 325 mg.

- Sodium: 281 mg.

- Carbohydrates: 52 g.

- Fiber: 2 g.

Protein: 10 g.

29.   Rich Chocolate Cookie

Preparation time: 10 minutes.

Cooking time: 9 minutes.

Servings: 4

Ingredients:

- Nonstick baking spray with flour

- 3 tablespoons softened butter

- ¹/3 cup plus 1 tablespoon brown sugar

- 1 egg yolk

- ½ cup flour

- 2 tablespoons ground white chocolate

- ¼ teaspoon baking soda

- ½ teaspoon vanilla

- ¾ cup chocolate chips

Directions:

- Select bake, set the temperature to 350°F (177°C) and set the time to 9 minutes. Select start/stop to begin preheating.

- In a prepared medium bowl, beat the butter and brown sugar together until fluffy. Stir in the egg yolk.

- Add the flour, white chocolate, baking soda, and vanilla, and mix well. Stir in the chocolate chips.

- Line a baking pan with parchment paper. Spray the parchment paper using a nonstick baking spray with flour.

- Spread the batter into the prepared pan, leaving a ½-inch border on all sides.

- Place the pan directly in the pot. Close the hood and bake for 9 minutes or until the cookie is light brown and just barely set.

- Get the pan from the grill and let cool for 10 minutes. Remove the cookie from the pan, remove the parchment paper, and let it cool on a wire rack.

- Serve immediately.

Nutrition:

- **Energy (calories):** 376

- **Protein:** 17.39g

- **Fat:** 15.53g

- **Carbohydrates:** 41.35g

30.   Lemony Blackberry Crisp

Preparation time: 5 minutes.

Cooking time: 20 minutes.

Servings: 1

Ingredients:

- 2 tablespoons lemon juice

- 1/3 cup powdered erythritol

- ¼ teaspoon xanthan gum

- 2 cup blackberries

- 1 cup crunchy granola

Directions:

- Select bake, set the temperature to 350°F (177°C) and set the time to 15 minutes. Select start/stop to begin preheating.

- In a bowl, combine the lemon juice, erythritol, xanthan gum, and blackberries. Transfer to a round baking pan and cover with aluminum foil.

- Place the pan directly in the pot. Close the hood and bake for 12 minutes.

- Take care when removing the pan from the grill. Give the blackberries a stir and top with the granola.

- Return the pan to the grill and bake at 320°F (160°C) for an additional 3 minutes. Serve once the granola has turned brown and enjoy.

Nutrition:

- **Ene**rgy (calories): 667

- Protein: 22.38g

- Fat: 12.06g

- Carbohydrates: 170.51g

CHAPTER 8:

Main Recipes

31.　　Air Fryer Ninja Foodi Eggplant

Preparation time: 10 minutes

Cooking time: 20 minutes

Servings: 2

Ingredients:

- 2 large eggplants

- 3 eggs beaten

- 1/3 cup Panko breadcrumbs

- 1 cup mozzarella cheese

- 2 cups of marinara sauce

- Olive oil spray

Directions:

1. Peel and slice the eggplants.

2. Take a shallow bowl and then place breadcrumbs in it.

3. Take a small bowl and scramble eggs in it.

4. Dip the eggplants first in the egg mixture and then dip them into breadcrumbs.

5. Preheat the Ninja Foodi for 5 minutes.

6. Spray the inner basket with canola oil spray.

7. Put eggplants inside and close the unit.

8. Select the air-crisp option and adjust temperate to 400 degrees F.

9. Set timer to 16 minutes.

10. After 12 minutes, open the unit and brush it with oil.

11. Cook for reaming 4 minutes.

12. Lay the slices of eggplants with mozzarella cheese.

13. Close the lid and select broil for a few minutes, about 2–4 minutes.

14. Then serve with marinara sauce.

Nutrition:

- Calories 570

% Daily Value*

- Total Fat 19 g 24% aturated Fat 6.2 g 31%

- Cholesterol 292 mg 97% Sodium 1227 mg 53%

- Total Carbohydrate 70.4 g 26% Dietary Fiber 25.9 g 93%

- Total Sugars 39.5 g

- Protein 23.8 g

32.   Pork Chops and Sage Sauce

Preparation time: 10 minutes

Cooking time: 15 minutes

Servings: 2

Ingredients:

- 1 shallot, sliced

- 1 tbsp. olive oil

- 2 tbsp. butter, melted

- 1 tsp. lemon juice

- 2 pork chops

- Salt and pepper as desired

- 1 handful sage, chopped

Directions:

1. Place the cooking pot into the Ninja Foodi AG301, and position the grill plate with the handles facing up.

2. Ensure the splatter shield is in position. Close the lid.

3. Press the GRILL button. Set the temperature to 370°F and adjust the time to 10 minutes. Press the START/STOP button to preheat the appliance for 8 minutes.

4. Season the pork with salt, pepper, and oil.

5. Transfer the pork to the grill plate and close the lid.

6. In a separate bowl, combine the butter, shallot, sage juice, and lemon juice.

7. Remove the grill plate, then add the sage mix to the cooking pot

8. Close the hood, press the bake button, set the timer for 5 minutes at the same temperature, and press the START button.

9. Drizzle pork with sage sauce.

Serving suggestions: Serve immediately.

Preparation and cooking tips: Flip the items on the grill plate halfway.

Nutrition:

- Calories: 265

- Fat: 6 g.

- Carb: 19 g.

- Proteins: 12 g.

33.   Smoked Ham Recipe

Preparation time: 5–10 minutes

Cooking time: 12–15 minutes

Servings: 4

Ingredients:

- 4 oz. smoked ham, scored

- 1/2 cup butter

- 2 tbsp. brown sugar

- 1 tbsp. honey

- 2 tbsp. pineapple cane syrup

Directions:

1. Place the grill rack inside the Ninja Foodi, pour a cup of water in it, and close the unit.

2. Let it preheat for 20 minutes at HIGH.

3. Meanwhile, melt butter in a cooking pot and add 2 tbsp. of brown sugar.

4. Melt it down and add a tbsp. of honey and pineapple cane syrup.

5. Mix well and let it get simmer until thickened.

6. Turn off the Ninja Foodi and open the unit.

7. Then brush the ham with glaze.

8. Close the unit and cook for 7 minutes.

9. After 5 minutes, open the unit by turning it off and glazed the ham again.

10. Cook for remaining 2 minutes

11. Sprinkle the ham with any favorite spice blend.

12. Slice and serve.

Nutrition:

- Calories: 291

- Fat: 25.5 g.

- Saturated Fat: 15.4 g.

- Cholesterol: 77 mg.

- Sodium: 535 mg.

- Carbohydrates: 12 g.

- Fiber: 0.5 g.

- Sugar: 10.7 g.

- Protein: 5 g.

34. Sweet Potato Casserole with Marshmallows

Preparation time: 10 minutes.

Cooking time: 33 minutes.

Servings: 8 to 10.

- 3 pounds (1.4 kilograms) sweet potatoes, peeled and cut into 1-inch cubes

- ½ cup of water

- Kosher salt to taste

- 1 cup packed light brown sugar

- 3 tablespoons butter, melted

- 1(½) teaspoon ground cinnamon

- 1 cup hot milk

- 2 cups mini marshmallows

- ½ cup pecans, chopped

Directions:

- Divide the sweet potatoes between two large pieces of foil, placing them in the center. Pour the water over the potatoes and season with salt. Wrap the foil around the potatoes, creating two pouches, and seal tightly. Place the foil packets on the sheet pan.

- Install a wire rack. Select bake, set the temperature to 400°F (204°C) and set the time to 30 minutes. Press start/stop to begin preheating.

- When the unit has preheated, place the sheet pan on the wire rack. Close the oven door to begin cooking.

- When cooking is complete, carefully transfer the potatoes to a large bowl. Add the brown sugar, butter, cinnamon, and milk. Using a fork or potato masher, you need to mash the sweet potatoes to your desired consistency.

- Transfer the potatoes to the casserole dish. Top them with marshmallows and pecans.

- Select broil, set the temperature to HI, and set the time to 3 minutes. Press start/stop to begin.

- Place the casserole dish on the wire rack and close the oven door to begin cooking.

- Cooking is done when the marshmallows are golden brown. Remove the dish from the oven and let it cool slightly before serving.

Nutrition:

- Energy (calories): 249

- Protein: 4.08g

- Fat: 4.78g

Carbohydrates: 49.62g

CHAPTER 9:

Sides Recipes

35.   Maple Candied Bacon

Preparation time: 5 minutes

Cooking time: 40 minutes

Servings: 12

Ingredients:

- ½ cup maple syrup

- ¼ cup brown sugar

- Nonstick cooking spray

- 1 pound (12 slices) thick-cut bacon

Directions:

1. Place the Reversible Rack in the pot. Close the Crisping Lid. Pre-heat the unit by selecting Air Crisp, setting the temperature to 400°F, and setting the time to 5 minutes.

2. In the meantime, in a small collaborating bowl, mix the maple syrup and brown sugar.

3. Once the Ninja Foodi has pre-heated, carefully line the Reversible Rack with aluminum foil. Spray the foil with cooking spray.

4. Arrange 4 to 6 slices of bacon on the rack in a single layer. Brush them with the maple syrup mixture.

5. Close the Crisping Lid. Select Air Crisp and set the temperature to 400°F. Fixed the time to 10 minutes, then choose Start/Stop to begin.

6. After 10 minutes, flip the bacon and brush with more maple syrup mixture. Adjust the Crisping Lid, select Air Crisp, fixed the temperature to 400°F, and set the time to 10 minutes. Select Start/Stop to begin.

7. Cooking is complete when your desired crispiness is reached. Remove the bacon from the Reversible Rack and transfer to a cooling rack for 10 minutes. Repeat steps 4 through 6 with the remaining bacon.

TIP: Do you like a little spice? Turn this recipe into a Spicy Maple Candied Bacon by adding ½ teaspoon of cayenne pepper to the maple-syrup-sugar mixture in step 2.

Nutrition:

- Calories: 451 Total fat: 34 g Saturated fat: 11 g

- Cholesterol: 51 mg Sodium: 634 mg Carbohydrates: 27 g

- Fiber: 0 g Protein: 9 g

36.   Snapper Fillets and Veggies

Preparation time: 10 minutes

Cooking time: 14 minutes

Servings: 2

Ingredients:

- 2 red snapper fillets, boneless

- 1/2 cup green bell pepper, chopped

- 1 tbsp. olive oil

- 1/2 cup red bell pepper, chopped

- 1/2 cup leeks, chopped

- Salt and black pepper as desired

- 1 tsp. tarragon, dried

- A splash of white wine

Directions:

1. Place the cooking pot into the Ninja Foodi AG301, and position the grill plate with the handles facing up.

2. Ensure the splatter shield is in position. Close the lid.

3. Press the GRILL button. Set the temperature to 350°F and adjust the time to 14 minutes. Press the START/STOP button to preheat the appliance for 8 minutes.

4. Season the fish with pepper, oil, salt, red bell pepper, green bell pepper, leeks, wine, and tarragon.

5. Transfer to the grill plate and close the lid.

6. Divide the fish and veggies into plates.

Serving suggestions: Serve immediately.

Preparation and cooking tips: Flip the items on the grill plate halfway.

Nutrition:

- Calories: 300

- Fat: 12 g.

- Carb: 29 g.

- Proteins: 12 g.

CHAPTER 10:

Poultry Recipes

37.   Orange Chicken and Broccoli

Preparation time: 15 minutes

Cooking time: 27 minutes

Servings: 2

Directions:

- 1 cup long-grain white rice

- 1 cup plus 2 tablespoons water

- 1 head broccoli, trimmed into florets

- 2 tablespoons extra-virgin olive oil, divided

- ¼ teaspoon of sea salt

- ¼ teaspoon freshly ground black pepper

- Nonstick cooking spray 4 boneless, skinless chicken tenders

- ¼ cup barbecue sauce ¼ cup sweet orange marmalade

- ½ tablespoon soy sauce

- 1 tablespoon sesame seeds for garnish

- 2 tablespoons sliced scallions for garnish

Directions:

1. Put the rice and water in the pot and stir to combine. Accumulate the Pressure Lid, making certain the pressure

release valve is in the Seal position. Select Pressure and set to High. Set the time to 2 minutes, then select Start/Stop to begin.

2. Meanwhile, in a medium mixing bowl, toss the broccoli with 1 tablespoon of olive oil. Season with salt and black pepper.

3. When pressure cooking is thorough, quick release the pressure by touching the pressure release valve to the vent position. Carefully remove the cover when the pressure has complete releasing.

4. Place the Reversible Rack inside the pot over the rice, making sure the rack is in the higher position. Spray the rack with nonstick cooking spray. Place the chicken tenders on the rack and brush them with the remaining 1 tablespoon of olive oil. Arrange the broccoli around the chicken tenders.

5. Close the Crisping Lid. Select Air Crisp, set the temperature to 400°F and set the time to 10 minutes. Press Start/Stop to begin.

6. Meanwhile, in a medium mixing bowl, stir together the barbecue sauce, orange marmalade, and soy sauce until well combined.

7. When Air Crisping is complete, coat the chicken with the orange sauce. Use tongs to flip the chicken and coat the other side. Close the Crisping Lid. Select Broil and set the time to 5 minutes. Select Start/Stop to begin.

8. After cooking is complete, check for your desired crispiness and remove the rack from the pot. The chicken is cooked when its internal temperature reaches 165°F on a meat thermometer.

9. Garnish with the sesame seeds and scallions and serve.

Nutrition:

- Calories: 849

- Total fat: 23 g

- Saturated fat: 3 g

- Cholesterol: 32 mg

- Sodium: 1057 mg

- Carbohydrates: 136 g

- Fiber: 12 g

- Protein: 31 g

38.   Delicious Whole Chicken

Preparation time: 10 minutes

Cooking time: 22 minutes

Servings: 4

Ingredients:

- 1 tsp. ground cumin

- 1/2 tbsp. fresh rosemary, minced

- 1 tsp. cayenne pepper

- Salt and black pepper to taste

- 1 tbsp. olive oil

- 1 tsp. red pepper flakes, crushed

- 1 lb. organic whole chicken, neck, and giblet removed

Directions:

1. Select the GRILL button on the Ninja Foodi Smart XL Grill and regulate MED settings for 25 minutes.

2. Mingle the rosemary, ground cumin, cayenne pepper, red pepper flakes, salt, and black pepper in a bowl.

3. Scrub the chicken with the spice mixture and olive oil.

4. Throw in the remaining ingredients and toss thoroughly.

5. Arrange the chicken in the Ninja Foodi when it displays ADD FOOD.

6. Grill for about 25 minutes and dole out on a platter.

7. Slice the chicken as you desire and serve.

Serving suggestions: Serve and enjoy with honey glazed veggies.

Variation tip: Select the whole chicken with a pinkish hue which shows fresh meat.

Nutrition:

- Calories: 207

- Fat: 7 g.

- Sat Fat: 1.4 g.

- Carbohydrates: 1 g.

- Fiber: 0.5 g.

- Sugar: 0.1 g.

- Protein: 33.1 g.

39.   Generous Hot Pepper Wings

Preparation time: 10 minutes

Cooking time: 25 minutes

Servings: 4

Ingredients:

- 1/2 tsp. paprika

- 1 tbsp. ranch salad dressing

- 1 lb. chicken wings

- 1 tbsp. coconut oil

- 2 tbsp. butter, melted

- 1/2 cup hot pepper sauce

Directions:

1. Take a mixing bowl and add oil, chicken, ranch dressing, paprika, and mix well.

2. Let it chill for 30–60 minutes.

3. Take another bowl and add pepper sauce, butter.

4. Pre-heat Ninja Foodi by demanding the GRILL option and situation it to MED and timer to 25 minutes.

5. Let it pre-heat till you hear a beep.

6. Arrange chicken wings over grill grate, lock lid, and let it cook until the timer runs out.

7. Serve chicken warm with pepper sauce.

8. Enjoy!

Nutrition:

- Calories: 510

- Carbohydrates: 6 g.

- Fat: 24 g.

- Protein: 54 g.

40. Crunchy Munchy Chicken Tenders with Peanuts

Preparation Time: 25 m

Cooking Time: 20 m

Servings: 4

Ingredients:

1. 1 ½ pounds chicken tenderloin

2. 2 tablespoons peanut oil

3. 1/2 cup tortilla chips, crushed

4. Sea salt and ground black pepper

5. 1/2 teaspoon garlic powder

6. 1 teaspoon red pepper flakes

7. 2 tablespoons peanuts, roasted and roughly chopped

Directions:

1. Start by preheating your Ninja Foodi Smart XL to 360 ° F.

2. Brush the chicken tenderloins with peanut oil on all sides.

3. In a mixing bowl, thoroughly combine the crushed chips, salt, black pepper, garlic powder, and red pepper flakes. Dredge the chicken in the breading, shaking off any residual coating.

4. Lay the chicken tenderloins into the cooking basket. Cook for 12 to 13 minutes or until it is no longer pink in the center. Work in batches; an instant-read thermometer should read at least 165 ° F.

5. Serve garnished with roasted peanuts. Bon appétit!

Nutrition:

- Calories 343

- Fat 16.4 g

- Carbs 10.6 g

- Protein 36.8 g

Conclusion

With the Ninja Foodie XL Grill Cookbook, you'll learn how to prepare the freshest food any way you like. You'll start with the basics and work your way up to more advanced techniques. With each technique, you'll get step-by-step instructions and helpful hints to make sure your foods turn out just right. Final Ninja Foodie XL Grill Tips:

- If you're new to grilling, start with the basics—the recipes are written for someone with minimal grilling experience.
- If you're a more advanced griller, feel free to use the recipes as a guide and make your own modifications.
- When you're grilling, always keep in mind that safety is the most important thing—if it seems like a recipe may be too complicated or you're not in a position to grill safely, then don't.
- Remember to grill in moderation and always have plenty of water on hand.
- Don't underestimate your Ninja Foodie XL Grill, especially when grilling.
- Have fun and enjoy the summer!

Tired of bland, boring grilled food? The Ninja Foodie XL Grill Cookbook is the perfect way to kickstart your grilling abilities. With great teaching tools like photos with every recipe and a large variety of recipes that range from basic to advanced and everything in between, you'll be well on your way to becoming a ninja griller.

If you own a Ninja Foodie XL Grill Cookbook, then you already know that it's more than just a grill cookbook. You've probably used it in ways that we never imagined. For instance, you may have used it to make "kabobs" by simply placing the meat on a skewer and cooking it on the grill. That's right! You just placed the meat on a skewer and cooked it!

But there's even more to the Ninja Foodie XL Grill Cookbook than this. You can use the cookbook to start your restaurant using your Ninja Foodie XL Grill Cookbook as a menu. You can even make food for customers right in your kitchen and then have them take it back to their homes with their own Ninja Foodie XL Grill Cookbook. This grill is for everyone no matter if he/she is a professional chef or a person who has just started to cook and wants to cook healthy food with no artificial preservatives added. Ninja Foodi Smart XL Grill is easy to use and will help you prepare your favorite recipes in minutes. It will inspire you to try new recipes as well. This grill comes with an excellent customer support service that will answer any question you might have within 24 hours. A smart grill that promises to cook food faster which is safer and healthier, enter the world of technology. From the name itself, Ninja Foodi Smart XL Grill is a grill that is smart and promises convenient for everyone to use. With this grill, it claims to cook meat in a healthy manner by emitting infrared heat from its dome-shaped lid. It sizzles the meat while leaving moisture and then results in a juicy flavor.

You can also use your Ninja Foodie XL Grill Cookbook to barbecue animals such as turkeys, chickens, and ducks on your grill. And you can roast marshmallows on your grill using your Ninja Foodie XL Grill Cookbook. You'll find all the Ninja Foodie XL Grill Cookbook tools that are necessary to do so inside of this cookbook! In conclusion, if you own a Ninja Foodie XL Grill Cookbook, then you'll see that it's more than just a grill cookbook; it's a tool that will allow you to experience many cooking techniques that we could never have imagined!

CPSIA information can be obtained
at www.ICGtesting.com
Printed in the USA
LVHW080502120521
687183LV00005B/497

9 781801 824316